T0123193

Will Ukraine Bloom Again?

STEPHAN A. DZEROVYCH

authorHOUSE®

AuthorHouse™
1663 Liberty Drive
Bloomington, IN 47403
www.authorhouse.com
Phone: 1 (800) 839-8640

Published by AuthorHouse 05/24/2017

ISBN: 978-1-5246-9088-5 (sc)
ISBN: 978-1-5246-9086-1 (hc)
ISBN: 978-1-5246-9087-8 (e)

Library of Congress Control Number: 2017907592

Print information available on the last page.

CONTENTS

Foreword....vii

Introduction....1

History Of Ukraine....11

- Early Times....11
- 3000 BC - 200 BC Period....12
- 200 BC - 850 AD Period....14
- Kievan Rus Period [850-1360]....15
- Period of Polish-Lithuanian and Russian Rule [1360-1795] Rise and Fall of Cossacks....21
- Period of Russian Tsarist and Austrian/Austro-Hungarian Rule [1795-1914]....33
- Ukraine during World War I [1914-1918]....39
- Ukraine in Aftermath of World War I [1918-1939]....44
- Ukraine during World War II [1939-1945]....46
- Ukraine after World War II [1945-1991]....51
- Ukraine since Independence [1991-Present]....54

What Went Wrong?....67

Will Ukraine Bloom Again?....73

Appendix I 81
Appendix II..85
Sources 87
About The Author 89

FOREWORD

The author of this book was born and lived in the Ukraine for the first ten years of his life. During this time he witnessed much destruction and acts of inhumanity as the ravages of World War II swept across Ukraine. Most of the book deals with the history of Ukraine, prompted by his desire to better understand his ancestors and their actions during the course of Ukraine's history.

Ukraine's proclamation of independence in 1991 brought joy and hope to Ukrainians around the world. However, its revival didn't go as well as expected.

The concluding section of the book looks into Ukraine's future and tries to answer the question on the minds of many Ukrainians: "Will Ukraine bloom again?"

I hope the reader will find the book educational and interesting.

INTRODUCTION

The objective of the introduction is to broadly familiarize the reader with Ukraine, particularly its geography, people, government, economy and political complexity.

The name Ukraine is derived from the Slavic word "kraj" meaning "land" or "borderland".

Not too long ago most people in the United States had difficulty finding Ukraine on the world map. The most often asked question of an Ukrainian national was: "Where is Ukraine?" Some thought it was still part of Russia. Others, more familiar with world geography and politics, saw it as a controversial place of discord and uncertainty divided into "East" and "West" blocs.

Today, after the violent Euromaidan revolution which resulted in the removal of President Victor Yanukovych from office by the Ukrainian Parliament on February 22, 2014, and the subsequent annexation of Crimea by Russia, as well as the rise of a separatist movement by pro-Russian rebels in its eastern regions, collectively known as Donbas, Ukraine is frequently in the news and has established a world wide identity. In fact, Ukraine has become an area of intense confrontation between the western powers of the United States and the European Union [EU] on one hand, and Russia on the other.

Located in Southeast Europe, Ukraine, particularly its central and southern areas, consists largely of very fertile plains known as steppe. A train ride from Lviv in the west to the capital Kiev in the central part of Ukraine gives the passenger a six hour almost uninterrupted view of agricultural fields occasionally crossed by brooks and rivers. The northern part of Ukraine has forested areas and the southwest is the most scenic, containing the Carpathian Mountains. Most of the south borders on the Black Sea and the Sea of Azov. [See Figure 1 - Map of Ukraine]

Figure 1 - Map of Ukraine

Ukraine is richly endowed with chernozem [black soil], one of the most fertile soils worldwide. Chernozem is a black colored soil that contains a high percentage of humus [10 percent or more] along with phosphorous and ammonia needed for enhanced plant growth. Ukraine also has a favorable climate for large scale agriculture and abundant water resources. About 50 percent of the country's total area is agricultural land, with agriculture amounting to about 10 percent of the national Gross Domestic Product [GDP] and employing a quarter of the working population. Among the leading crops are wheat, maize, barley, sunflower, beets, fruits and vegetables.

Ukraine has a large supply of mineral and raw material resources including iron, coal, manganese, titanium and uranium ore. Its diversified industrial sector includes machine building, metalworking, power generation, ship building and mining. Much of Ukraine's industry is concentrated in the Donbas region where rich coal and iron ore deposits are located. Some of this eastern area is currently under the control of the separatists.

Total population of Ukraine is about 42.5 million [excluding Crimea]. Kiev is the capital with a population of almost 3 million. Bisected by the Dnieper River and located on its hilly shores, Kiev is a picturesque and colorful city with wide tree-lined streets, numerous parks, monuments, historical buildings, museums and churches. [See Appendix I] The central part of Kiev is situated on a hill with St. Sophia's Cathedral and the nearby Opera

House on its top. From there, streets run downhill to other parts of central Kiev. On the eastern side, they connect with Khreshchatyk Street [Kiev's main street] on which the Maidan [City Square], the Independence Monument and Kiev's City Hall are located. At its end, the street connects with Kiev's business district. Some of Kiev's streets are still cobble stone covered and outdoor cafes are abundant, with menus predominated by Ukrainian dishes including varenyky [potato dumplings-pierogis], holubtsi [stuffed cabbage rolls] and borshch [red beet root soup]. The Kiev Metro System is the city's main mode of public transportation. Modern and mostly underground, it has over 50 stations and three lines that meet in the center of the city near Khreshchatyk Street. Buses running along main streets provide additional transportation.

Other large cities are Kharkiv in the northeast [pop. 1.4 million], Odessa in the south on the Black Sea [pop. 1 million], Dnipropetrovsk [pop. 1 million] in central Ukraine, Donetsk [pop. .95 million] in the east and Lviv [pop. .75 million] in the west.

Ukrainians living in the western parts of Ukraine have a predominantly western European orientation. Those living in the east and south, having been under Russian rule for long periods, are for the most part socially and politically closer to Russia.

Most people in the Kiev region speak the modern Ukrainian language [used in government and schools], and public signs are in Ukrainian. However, sometimes Russian words find their way into the vocabulary. Western Ukrainians [in Lviv and surrounding areas] also speak the modern Ukrainian language, however, again there is some influence of the Polish and German vocabulary as a result of the Polish and Austro-Hungarian rule over western Ukraine in the past. In the eastern and southern regions, Russian, or a mixture of Russian and Ukrainian, is the prevalent language of the population. However, the use of the modern Ukrainian language is increasing.

Ukraine is a predominantly Christian nation, with religion playing an important part in Ukrainian society. As with language, the practice of religion is split between western, central and eastern parts of Ukraine. The religion of the majority of people living in the west is Greek Catholicism. Overall about 15 percent of Ukrainians who practice religion are Greek Catholic. The Greek Catholic Church was established in 1596 and recognizes the Pope as spiritual leader, but uses eastern Orthodox rites. The central region, including Kiev, is predominated by the Ukrainian Orthodox Church of Kiev Patriarchate, and the eastern and southern regions are mostly of the Ukrainian Orthodox Church of what is referred to as Moscow Patriarchate. The Kiev Patriarchate was formed after Ukraine achieved independence from Russia in 1991 and has about a 40 percent participation of religious people in all of Ukraine. About 30 percent of the Ukrainian religious population is Ukrainian Orthodox of the Moscow Patriarchate. It enjoys a self-governing status within the Moscow Patriarchate and is virtually independent in all administrative matters. A much smaller percentage of the religious population also practices the Ukrainian Autocephalous Orthodox, the Protestant, the Roman Catholic, the Islamic and Jewish religions.

The Ukrainian economy took a dramatic downturn in 2015 as a result of the post-Euromaidan hostilities in the country. The harsh recession in 2015 lowered the GDP to about 87 billion [US$], which ranked only 70th among the nations of the world. The economy remains in poor state due to underdeveloped infrastructure, bureaucracy, corruption and political turmoil. Inflation is near 10 percent. The average minimum wage is about $.75 per hour and the average yearly net salary is about $2800. Pensions for people over 60 years old is about $75 per month. Unemployment is near 10 percent and almost 25 percent of the population is below the poverty line. While 2017 has seen some improvement in the economy, the overall progress has been slow and not uniform. The Ukrainian currency is the Hryvnia which has an exchange rate of about 26 Hryvnia to 1 US$.

Faced with a weak economy and a conflict in the east of the country, Ukraine elected Petro Poroshenko President on May 25, 2014. A former Minister of Foreign Affairs from 2009-2010 and a Minister of Trade and Economic Development in 2012, Poroshenko has been a prominent oligarch and business man. He owns a large scale confectionary company Roshen, which earned him the nickname "Chocolate King". The President is also the leader of the Petro Poroshenko Bloc Party which advocates decentralization in Ukraine but opposes federalization, reflecting the President's views.

Ukraine is a Republic with the President and Prime Minister possessing executive powers. The Verkhovna Rada [Parliament] with 450 elected members holds legislative powers. While the President is responsible for selecting the Prime Minister and cabinet, it requires the approval of the Verkhovna Rada. Ukraine is also a multiparty country with many parties forming coalitions at election time.

The Armed Forces of Ukraine are composed of the Ground Forces, the Navy, the Air Force and the Airmobile Forces. Total active personnel is about 250,000. Since June 3, 2016, women are allowed to serve in combat units of the Armed Forces of Ukraine.

Despite the harsh economic conditions and the conflict in the east of the country, life of Ukrainians in the western and central regions, at least on the surface, appears to go on normally. In the eastern regions, particularly near the areas of the conflict, conditions are substantially worse. Occasional flare-ups of fighting between the Ukrainian Army and separatists is common.

In Kiev, people rush to work in the morning on well-kept subways and busses, young people go to school, mothers with young children and older people fill the parks' benches, and cafes are fairly full, especially during lunch hours. Some, who can't find steady jobs, sell ice cream, coffee, fruits and flowers on street corners, in parks and Metro hallways. Streets in Ukrainian cities are clean and most buildings are well kept. The worse economically affected areas appear to be in the rural regions with many homes in need of repair. Most streets, even in the bigger cities like Kiev, Kharkiv, Odessa and Lviv, are relatively quiet and empty after midnight, reflecting the unsettled economic and political situation in the country. However, night life, particularly in Kiev on weekends, goes on into the morning hours with dancing and shows in several of the city's night clubs, which demonstrates the enthusiasm and optimism of the younger generation. Crime in Ukraine is only moderate and use of drugs is low.

Despite the outward appearance of normal life in Ukraine, there is a discernable underlying tension that one can sense among the population, particularly increasing as one goes from west to east. One can sense that the country is not fully settled yet. This sense of insecurity is demonstrated to some extent by the empty streets in the late evening hours and the presence of private security guards in many establishments.

Much has changed since the author left Ukraine in 1949. However, as in the past, the Ukrainian people are friendly, hospitable and cheerful with a touch of stubbornness and trickery, which probably prevents them from reaching a compromise in the standoff with the eastern rebels. Ukrainians value their own opinions and tend to take a firm stand on their convictions, especially when it comes to politics. Criticism of their own government is forceful and abundant. Ukrainians are hard working and build strong families. Many receive their strength from deep religious beliefs. Churches are full even during services on weekdays. In colorful Orthodox rite services the entire congregation tends to join in a chorus of religious and patriotic songs asking God to bless Ukraine in its greatest need.

There were periods in Ukrainian history when Ukrainian culture and customs experienced considerable influences of other cultures such as those of Byzantium, Greece and Vikings, but it basically preserved its general original quality.

One such custom that survived since Ukraine's pagan times is the art of painting eggs [pysanky] associated with Easter. The word pysanka is derived from the Ukrainian word pysaty [to write]. The symbols used in pysanka are a blend of ancient pagan motifs with Christian elements. The Ukrainian pagans celebrated the high points in life and the yearly cycle beginning with the arrival of Spring. The Christians similarly highlighted the Spring and the resurrection of Christ at Easter time. Thus in spite of its turbulent and dramatic history, Ukrainian culture including a wide spectrum of art, literature, folk music, embroidery and native customs was always preserved beginning from the early times of its existence.

Another traditional Ukrainian custom that goes back many centuries is to greet visitors with bread [representing hospitality] and salt [representing friendship]. Additionally, to get everyone in a good mood, a toast to good health [na zdorovja] is usually offered. But the one thing you must avoid is to shake hands across the threshold of a door, as it is considered bad luck.

HISTORY OF UKRAINE

Early Times
Miocene, Pliocene and Pleistocene Periods

During the Miocene geological period, some 15 million years ago, most of Ukraine was covered by sea. Toward the end of this period, about ten million years ago, the seas receded to the approximately present day coasts of Black, Azov and Caspian seas to form one big sea. The climate was warm and humid. Lush vegetation covered the ground and large animals roamed the land.

Then some 5 million years ago, during the Pliocene geological period, the climate began to cool. Many plants and animals disappeared and only those, which could adapt to lower temperatures, such as fury animals, remained. As the climate cooled further about 1 million years ago during the Pleistocene Period, commonly known as the Ice Age, the ground froze up and ice sheets covered most of the northern parts of Ukraine.

When the ice retreated, life started to reappear. Traces of human habitation in Ukraine, dating back at least 30 thousand years, became evident as a result of geological excavations. Primitive stone tools, carvings from mammoth tusks, arrowheads made from flint stone, earthenware, bronze tools and gold jewelry found in different layers of earth enabled geologists to reconstruct the way of life of early Ukrainian man. The evidence indicates that they at first relied mostly on hunting and fishing for existence. Then gradually, they began to make utensils, kept domestic animals, constructed dwellings and cultivated the soil.

3000 BC - 200 BC Period

The first known inhabitants of southern and central Ukraine were a pastoral and agricultural people, part of a culture that inhabited the area east and north of the Black Sea around 3000 BC. Most settlements were in the regions of the wooded steppe along the Dnieper, Bug and Dniester Rivers. Some of the larger villages contained as many as one to two hundred huts arranged in concentric circles with walls made of wattle and clay supported by close-set timbers. A middle-sized hut contained two separate rooms. Clay ovens were used for cooking and warming the huts in the winter. Agriculture was based on cultivation of wheat, barley and corn. These early farmers also bred cattle, horses, goats and pigs. Starting around 1000 BC, the southern and central Ukrainian steppe was successively invaded for the next

800 years by related tribes who came from Central Asia and spoke different dialects of the Indo-Iranian language. Unlike their predecessors who were agricultural people, these tribes were nomadic, generally moving over long periods from east to west. In many instances a stronger tribe ruled over other tribes in a feudal fashion. The movement of these tribes call to mind a billiard table on which one ball strikes another and stops, as it puts the other in motion. Some of the better known tribes were the Cimmerians [circa 900 BC], the Scythians [from about 800 BC] and Sarmatians [circa 300 BC].

The first to infiltrate the Ukrainian steppe were mounted nomads known as Cimmerians who came from northern Iran. These mounted horsemen eventually became dominant on the steppe and subjugated the ancient pastoral people.

Sometime around 800 BC, another horse-back riding nomadic tribe, related to the Cimmerians and known as Scythians, moved westward from Central Asia and pushed the Cimmerians out. The Scythians, a savage, warlike tribe with tattooed bodies depicting real and imaginary beasts, were skilled horsemen and archers. They also used horse drawn covered wagons and maintained well traveled routes that connected their settlements. At their height around 500 BC, the Scythians controlled most of the area of modern Ukraine. They spoke the Indo-Iranian language, but had no system of writing. They rode horses with no stirrups or saddles [only saddle cloths] and their garments were of padded and quilted leather with trousers tucked into short boots, open tonics and pointed hoods. Scythian women dressed in much the same fashion as the men and at times fought alongside of them in battle. The burial of the tribe's chief was an elaborate mourning ceremony. The corpse, embalmed in wax and aromatic herbs and laid on a horse-drawn bier, would be taken on a solemn procession through the dead chief's territory. The Scythians dominated the Ukrainian steppe north of the Black Sea until about 300 BC, when a kindred tribe, the Sarmatians, moved in from Central Asia and started to push the Scythians from the steppe.

By 200 BC, the Sarmatians gained control over most of the area. The impact of the Scythians and the Sarmatians on the Slavonic people living in adjacent areas to the north was important and lasting, and the vocabulary of the Slavonic languages comprises many words of the Scythian/ Sarmatian origin.

200 BC - 850 AD Period

At about the same time as the Sarmatians controlled the southern areas of Ukraine [circa 200 BC], the Slavs started to become prominent in the marshes bordering today's Belarus. The Slavs, a sedentary, agricultural people who spoke a branch of the Indo-European language occupied a large area in northern Europe stretching from the Dnieper to the Vistula Rivers. There they were exposed to various cultural influences from the Baltic tribes in the north, the Scythians/Sarmatians from the south and the Goths from the west. From about 150 AD, the Slavic tribes began to expand in all directions. Some set out to the west reaching the Elbe River and became ancestors of the Czechs, Slovaks and Poles. Others moved south and became known as Serbs, Croats, Slovaks, Macedonians and Montenegrins. Others moved northwest and became Lithuanians, Latvians and Estonians. The last group, the East Slavs, remained in generally the same area what is now Belarus, Ukraine and Western Russia. Over time many ethnically diverse nomadic peoples migrated into this region or occupied it for long periods [Goths circa 100 AD], [Huns circa 370 AD], [Avers circa 600 AD], Khazars [circa 700 AD]. However, the East Slavs remained and eventually became dominant.

Kievan Rus Period [850-1360]

By the 9th century, Scandinavian people known as Varangians began to penetrate through the Baltic regions into Eastern Europe. Rurik, the leader of the Varangians, some of whom were also known as Rus, established himself in Novgorod [currently northwest Russia] around 860. In the 870's, Oleg succeeded Rurik as leader of the Varangians at Novgorod. Under Oleg the Varangians made their way south along the Dnieper River and around 879 settled in Kiev, thus establishing the State of Kievan Rus. Oleg made Kiev his capital and set out to unite the Slavic tribes along the Dnieper waterway, freeing them around 910 from the overlordship of the Khazars. He conducted military expeditions to the shores of the Caspian Sea and concluded commercial treaties with the Byzantine Empire, making trade with the empire a major factor in the Kievan economy. His dealings with the Byzantineans opened the way to Greek cultural penetration of Kievan Rus, as Greece at that time was part of the Byzantine Empire. In 912, Oleg was succeeded by Rurik's son Igor. Many of Igor's military campaigns were not successful and in 945 he was killed by the Derivians, a rebellious Slavic tribe, while collection tribute. After Igor's death, his wife Olga served as regent for their son Sviatoslav until he came of age in 962. She is known for her obliteration of the Derivians, the tribe that killed her husband. Before she came into power, Kievan Rus was a pagan society. In 964, Olga went to Constantinople and while there she converted to Christianity, being baptized by the Patriarch [the highest figure in the Eastern Church] with the Roman Emperor Constantine VII himself as the Godfather. Despite her urgings, her son refused to convert, although he did not oppose the new religion. She apparently had a huge influence, however, on her grandson Vladimir the Great who in 988 made Christianity the official religion of Kievan Rus. In 1547, the Orthodox Church named Olga of Kiev a Saint and an equal to the Apostles. In 964, Olga established her son Sviatoslav on the throne.

Sviatoslav was an able and courageous prince who fought Asian hordes in the east and Bulgarians in the west. He divided his state between his sons which allowed him to continue his expeditions and battles. When he died in 972 during a battle with the Pechenegs, a central Asia semi-nomadic Turkic tribe, his sons fought between themselves for control of Kievan Rus.

In 980, Prince Vladimir, Sviatoslav's youngest son, defeated all his brothers, and unified the country into one powerful state with Kiev as its capital. This signaled the beginning of the Golden Age of Kievan Rus. Vladimir continued to expand his territories beyond his father's extensive domain and build numerous fortresses to protect the state. During his reign he conquered and united distant Slavic tribes and waged successful wars on the Lithuanians, the Bulgars, the Pechenegs and the Byzantines in Crimea. Vladimir produced silver and gold coins with his portrait on one side and the trident on the other side. The Trident is the coat of arms of present day Ukraine. Originally a pagan, Vladimir adopted Christianity in 988, probably influenced by the political and economic advantages of an alliance with Christian Byzantium. His baptism in 988 was followed by his marriage to Anna, sister of the Byzantine Emperor Basil II. After the wedding he returned Crimea to Byzantium. Vladimir renounced his pagan ways and made Greek Orthodox Christianity the religion of his people. He started to convert the population, which had up to then worshipped pagan gods, and in the process many inhabitants of Kiev were baptized. Vladimir devoted the remainder of his life to building churches, including the splendid Cathedral of Tithes [989] in Kiev, and the establishment of schools and libraries.

After Vladimir's death in 1015, fighting and assassinations between his sons ensued, resulting in victory of Prince Yaroslav over his brother Sviatopolk in 1019. A shrewd statesman, known as Yaroslav the Wise, he further consolidated the power and prestige of the Kievan Rus. He regained West Halychyna [Galicia] from the Poles, crushed the nomadic invaders Pachenegs and suppressed rebellions by Lithuanian and Finnish tribes. At home he encouraged learning, codified laws, erected magnificent buildings and churches, including the famous Cathedral of St. Sophia in Kiev. Yaroslav was in close contact with European dynasties and his daughters were married to Harold III of Norway, Andrew I of Hungary and Henry I of France. During his lengthy reign [1019-1054], Kievan Rus reached the zenith of its cultural splendor and military power. Before his death in 1054, Yaroslav divided his kingdom between his heirs designating the oldest, Iziaslav I, as Grand Duke of Kiev. The others were told to obey Iziaslav as they had their father, but civil war ensued and Kievan Rus split into principalities.

In 1054, the eastern and western churches separated [known as the East West Schism], as the western regions of Ukraine became the focus of intense rivalry between Roman Catholicism and Eastern Orthodoxy. This religious rivalry created a divide between the eastern and western parts of Ukraine which still exists today.

In 1097, the princes of the various principalities agreed to stop fighting between themselves, and in 1103 they united their forces under the leadership of Prince Monomakh, a grandson of Yaroslav the Great. After his death in 1125, Ukraine again broke up into numerous principalities with only nominal allegiance to the Prince of Kiev, occupied by sons of Monomakh on rotational basis. When Yurij Dolgorukiy, the Prince of Kiev and one of Monomakh's sons, died in 1157, his son Andrey Bogolyubsky did not take up his father's throne in Kiev, but rather remained as Prince of Vladimir. Andrey tried to unite the Kievan Rus lands, including Kiev and Novgorod under his authority. However, pursuing such a policy led Andrey to bitter disputes with Kiev. In 1169, Andrey attacked and conquered Kiev. Much of the city was destroyed and residents were taken captive as slaves to Vladimir. He then established his capital in Vladimir, near the present site of Moscow, thus originating the current Russian State.

By the year 1200, Kievan Rus was divided into three centers of power, Halychyna and Volhynia in the west near Poland, the trade city of Novgorod in the north and Vladimir in the forests of northeast. The western parts of Ukraine, Halychyna and Volhynia, gradually emerged as the leading principalities. Prince Roman ruled there in 1199 and his sons succeeded in uniting both principalities into one rich and powerful state.

About the year 1223, hordes of Mongols and Tartars started to invade parts of Kievan Rus. Some princes of what remained of Kievan Rus united and fought together to expel this new horde. After defeating the combined armies of Kiev and Halychyna, the Mongol forces retreated probably to plan for the successor to Genghis Khan, the founder of the Mongol Empire who died in 1227. About 14 years later, the Mongol armies returned under the leadership of Batu Khan. In the campaigns of 1238-1240 they swept away most of Kievan Rus, burned cities and killed great numbers of the population including the ruling houses and the church hierarchy. The Mongols imposed taxes and laws, often raiding towns to suppress rebellions. Between 1250 and 1300, the eastern principalities of Kievan Rus experienced periods of submission alternating with rebellion. Yet the culture and people survived despite vassalage to the Mongol Golden Horde.

In the west, Poland in 1349 managed to occupy parts of Halychyna and Volhynia. At about the same time, Lithuanian princes intensified their takeover of eastern principalities of Kievan Rus weakened by Mongol invasions. Finally about the year 1360, the Prince of Kiev was overthrown by Algirdas, the Grand Duke of Lithuania, thus essentially ending what was left of Kievan Rus.

From here on the eastern and western regions of Kievan Rus have separate histories. Due to the fact that the political and cultural core of Kievan Rus was located on the territory of modern Ukraine, Ukrainian historians and scholars consider Kievan Rus to be the founding of the Ukrainian State. This is also the position of the author of this book. Russian historians, on the other hand, consider Kievan Rus the first period of Russian history. Furthermore, all historical events described from here on that occurred on territories of modern Ukraine will be treated as having occurred in Ukraine.

Period of Polish-Lithuanian and Russian Rule [1360-1795] Rise and Fall of Cossacks

After the breakup of Kievan Rus, by about the middle of the 14th century, today's Ukrainian territories came under the rule of the Kingdom of Poland, the Grand Duchy of Lithuania, and the Tatar Golden Horde of Mongolia.

During the rule of King Casimir III Poland expanded further to the east and, starting by about 1360, occupied some of the former regions of Kievan Rus including all of Halychyna and Volhynia. These areas are part of today's western and northwestern Ukraine including the city of Lviv located in Halychyna. Under Polish rule these regions were subjected to exploitation and colonization by influx of Polish, German and Jewish peoples who took over the properties and offices from local boyars, members of Ukraine's highest level of society and state administrations. Catholic Poland also exerted enormous pressure on the Orthodox population to accept Catholicism.

About the same time, Lithuanian princes intensified their takeover of former Kievan Rus eastern regions, which largely correspond to today's central and eastern parts of Ukraine. By 1370's, most of the principalities of these regions, including Kiev, came under the control of Algirdas, the Grand Duke of Lithuania. The Lithuanian State of the late 14th century became primarily binominal consisting of Lithuania and former Kievan Rus principalities corresponding to modern Ukraine and Belarus.

The Lithuanian princes were just rulers and Ukraine flourished under their rule. In many cases the Lithuanians were assimilated and they adopted the local customs, language and religion. The Ukrainian princes were Orthodox and many Lithuanian princes and nobles converted to Orthodoxy, even some that resided in Lithuania proper. The Ukrainian people did not resist the Lithuanian rulers and they appreciated their protection from Tartars in the south, Poland in the west and Moscow Duchy in the north. Historical territories of former principalities were mostly preserved and considerable autonomy was given to them under Lithuanian rule.

The Lithuanian rule over Ukrainian regions did not extend to cover the steppes bordering the Black Sea and Crimea. These regions continued to be ruled by the Mongolian Tatar Golden Horde. The Tatar rule was largely indirect, limited to extraction of taxes and tribute whose collection was delegated to local princes.

After Algirdas's death in 1377, Jogaila became the Grand Duke of Lithuania. In 1385, following the Act of Kreva, which laid out the Lithuanian-Polish Union, he converted to Catholicism. This allowed him to marry the 12-year old Catholic child Queen Jadviga of Poland the following year. As a result of this marriage Jogaila also became the King of Poland. The established Polish-Lithuanian union was ruled by the Jagiellon dynasty till 1572. Pressured by Poland, Jogaila ordered his court and followers to convert to Catholicism. Furthermore, in 1413, during the following rule of Lithuania by Grand Duke Vytautas, a decision was made to allow only Catholics to occupy important government positions. Nearly all Ukrainians, including princes and boyars, at that time were Orthodox. Wide-spread discrimination against the Orthodox population followed. Starting about 1490, some Ukrainians revolted against the increasingly harsh rule and others started to move to lower regions of Ukraine closer to the areas bordering the Black Sea, thus initiating the Cossack movement.

During the first half of the 16th century, Lithuania increasingly needed a closer alliance with Poland, as the Grand Duchy of Moscow threatened to recover the Orthodox ruled former lands of Kievan Rus. The Polish nobility, sensing a change in the balance of power of the union, demanded more equal and permanent arrangement with Lithuania. In 1569, with the Union of Lublin, Lithuania and Poland formed a new state referred to as the Polish-Lithuanian Commonwealth. The Commonwealth, which officially consisted of the Crown of the Kingdom of Poland and the Grand Duchy of Lithuania, was ruled by the Polish and Lithuanian nobility, together with nobility elected kings. The union was designed to have a common foreign policy, customs and currency. Separate Polish and Lithuanian armies were retained, but parallel ministerial and central administrative offices were established. The Commonwealth ruled Poland and Lithuania until 1795.

Under the Polish-Lithuanian Commonwealth, the Ukrainian lands formerly ruled by the Grand Duchy of Lithuania were incorporated into the Polish Crown. The settlement of Polish nationals on Ukrainian territories followed, and Polish laws and customs became dominant. Polish nobles replaced most of the Ukrainian princes and boyars. Peasants lost their land ownership and civil rights. They gradually became serfs, exploited in agriculture and forestry by the new landowners. Suppression of the Orthodox Church retarded the development of Ukrainian literature, arts and education. Preferential treatment of Catholics inhibited economical and political advancement of Ukrainians.

Eventually, the harsh conditions of Polish rule led many to flee serfdom and religious persecution by escaping beyond the area of the lower Dnieper rapids where some venturesome Ukrainians had moved earlier to be more independent. This area of Ukraine offered excellent opportunity for hunting, fishing and farming with abundance of very rich and productive soil. Over a period of time, this area north of the Black Sea attracted many adventurous Ukrainians. Even though they had to fight marauding Tatar hordes present in this region, they were free of serfdom and persecution of their Polish overlords. There they constructed forts called "sich" to defend themselves against the Tatars. They established a military order called Zaporozhian [clearing beyond the rapids] Sich [forts]. These fugitives became to be known as Cossacks, an adaptation of the Turkish word Kazak, meaning "outlaw" or "adventurer". At the end of the 16th century, the commander of the Cossacks, originally known as the starshyi [elder], became known as hetman [Polish word for leader]. Elected by and responsible to the Cossack Council called Rada, he had broad powers as the commander of the Cossack army.

With time the influx of Ukrainians to Cossack territory increased, their strength grew and they were able to drive away the Tatars into Crimea. The number of Cossacks fluctuated between 30 and 50 thousand. The growing number of independence-minded Cossacks started to concern Poland. The Polish rulers tried to control the Cossacks by recruiting some of them into the Polish military system as so called Registered Cossacks, but they were not very successful. With decreasing danger from the Tatars, Polish nobles and Ukrainian princes loyal to the Polish king were granted possessions in territories controlled by the Cossacks and began to introduce freedom limiting, unpopular laws. About 1591, dissatisfied with such treatment, the Cossacks under Hetman Kryshtof Kosynskyi rebelled and by year 1593 controlled large areas of eastern Ukraine. The revolt was eventually put down by the Polish military, but only with great difficulty.

In 1596, the Polish King, Sigmund III Vasa, ordered his commander to subjugate the Cossack forces. The Cossack fighters, heavily outnumbered, were put under a prolonged siege and suffered many casualties. However, some escaped to carry on the fight. In the same year, the Ukrainian Orthodox bishops, confronted with the power of Polish Catholicism, established the Uniate, or Greek Catholic Faith, which recognized papal authority but retained the Orthodox rites. This was not accepted well by the predominantly Orthodox Ukrainian population including the Cossack leadership.

Despite their differences with the Cossacks, Poland on occasions resorted to secure their help in fighting their neighboring states. In turn the Cossacks demanded compensation and better treatment. As a result, in 1603 the Cossacks obtained equal status with the Polish military units and secured authority over large area of Ukraine adjacent to the Dnieper River. However, during periods when the Poles were not endangered by their enemies, they again turned their attention to pacification of the Cossacks and demanded a reduction in the growing Cossack military force. The Polish king, although unable to suppress the Cossacks, continued with a policy of conversion of the Ukrainian population to Catholicism by persecution of people of the Orthodox faith. As the religious conflict raged on, in 1620 the entire Zaporozhian host joined the Kievan Orthodox Brotherhood. Thus, in the great religious divide, the Cossacks became identified with staunch support of Orthodoxy and uncompromising opposition to the Uniate church. Under the protection afforded by the Cossacks and the dynamic leadership of the new Metropolitan of Kiev Petro Mohyla, Orthodoxy flourished in Ukraine. It became the driving force behind a cultural revival that included the establishment of the Kiev Mohyla Academy, the first Ukrainian institution of higher learning.

As Poland made peace with its neighbors, the Cossack movement came under renewed pressure from its Polish rulers. In 1624, the Orthodox Church authorities asked Moscow for help, but Russia was not strong enough to get involved in hostilities with Poland. After another unsuccessful attempt to overthrow the Polish occupation was made by the Cossacks in 1638, the Cossack movement came under Polish control. Deprived of protection from the Cossacks, the peasants and city dwellers were reduced to poverty. Political, cultural and religious matters were under Polish control and commerce was predominantly in hands of Jewish merchants, storekeepers and innkeepers.

Tensions simmering from social discontent, religious strife and Cossack resentment of Polish authority finally coalesced and came to a head in 1648. Beginning with a seemingly typical Cossack revolt, under the leadership of Cossack Hetman Bohdan Khmelnytsky, Ukraine was soon involved in an unprecedented war and revolution. Khmelnytsky was a nobleman, who unable to obtain justice for wrongs suffered at Polish hands, fled to the Sich in late 1647 and was soon elected hetman. In this capacity he began preparations for an insurrection against the Polish rulers. In 1648, a Polish army send to forestall the rebellion was soundly defeated. The victory provided the impetus for a popular uprising. Violence spread throughout Ukraine as Cossacks and peasants vented their fury on those they associated with Polish tyranny and social oppression, including officials, landlords, Jewish merchants and Uniate clergy. The Poles, in turn, took bloody reprisals against the rebellious population. After more victories against Poland, in 1649 Khmelnytsky entered Kiev to triumphal acclaim as liberator. He further set out to establish Ukraine as an independent Cossack State. He created an administration under a new governing elite drawn from the Cossack officers and initiated relations with foreign states. Negotiations with Poland followed, but agreements reached were not acceptable to the Polish nobility, the Cossack leadership and the Ukrainian radicalized masses. As military operations continued inconclusively, Khmelnytsky began to look for allies and concluded a treaty with Moscow which accepted the tsar's suzerainty but provided for Ukraine's autonomy including an elective hetmancy, self-government and the right to conduct foreign relations. Moscow entered the war against Poland, but no decisive breakthrough resulted. Despite some joint victories, Khmelnytsky became increasingly disillusioned with the Moscow alliance caused by Russian interference in internal Ukrainian affairs. There were indications that the hetman planned to sever the Moscow tie, but died before he could do so.

Khmelnytsky's successor, Hetman Ivan Vyhovsky, broke with Moscow, and in 1658 concluded a new Treaty of Halychyna with Poland. By its terms, central Ukraine, including Kiev, was to constitute a self-governing Grand Duchy of Rus, joined with Poland and Lithuania as an equal member of a tripartite commonwealth. Unacceptable to both the Polish nobility and the Cossacks, the treaty was never implemented. Faced with mounting opposition, Vyhovsky resigned the hetmancy and fled to Poland.

After Vyhovsky, Ukraine began a rapid descent into chaos. Tensions increased between the Cossack officers, who were undergoing a transformation into the hereditary landowning class, and rank and file Cossacks as well as the peasantry who were expected to provide the labor. From 1663, rival hetmans rose and fell in the competing Polish and Russian spheres of influence. In 1667, by the Truce of Andrusovo between Russia and the Polish-Lithuanian Commonwealth, Ukraine was partitioned along the Dnieper River. The west, known as the Right Bank, reverted to Poland, while Russia received possession of the east, known as the Left Bank. Kiev, which was actually located on the Right Bank, also became Russia's possession. The arrangement was confirmed in 1686 by the Treaty of Eternal Peace between Poland and Russia.

The partition of Ukraine caused a patriotic reaction. The hetman of the Right Bank, Petro Doroshenko, briefly occupied the Left Bank and sought to recreate a unified Ukrainian State under the vassalage of the Ottoman

Empire. A massive Ottoman military intervention in 1672 resulted in the annexation of Podilia, a southern region of Ukraine stretching between the Dniester River in the east and the Carpathian Mountains in the west. Doroshenko's hopes and popularity evaporated as further Ottoman operations against Poland failed to establish his rule and led to devastation, especially after Russia was drawn into the war. Massive flight of the population to the Left Bank depopulated large areas of the Right Bank Ukraine. Two large scale Ottoman campaigns followed Doroshenko's abdication in 1676, but a truce in 1681 put an end to further direct Turkish military involvement. Ottoman power was soon on the wane in Europe, and in 1699 the province of Podilia reverted to Polish rule. This in effect ended the autonomous Hetman State in the Right Bank of Ukraine.

The society in the Right Bank in the 18th century differed markedly from the earlier period of the Hetmanate. The Cossacks virtually disappeared as a significant organized force. Cities and towns experienced a serious decline, and the population became more heavily Polish. The Uniate Church became predominant among Ukrainians, with Orthodoxy claiming a much smaller number of adherents. In the absence of a strong central authority with the elimination of the Cossacks as a counterbalancing force, the Right Bank became dominated by Polish nobility. Especially influential were a few aristocratic families whose huge estates formed virtually independent fiefdoms with their own privately armed militias.

Beginning with the middle of the 18th century, the Commonwealth of Poland and Lithuania started to unravel, as Russia started to exert pressure on the Commonwealth. During the Seven Year's War [1756-1763], initially between France and Great Britain, which eventually involved every European power of the time, Poland allowed Russian troops access to its western lands as bases. This came to exert pressure on Poland and its independence. Over time Russia was able to control the Polish nobility and even dictated the terms of the new Polish constitution. Deep resentment of Russian intervention in Poland's domestic affairs led to the War of Confederation of Bar [1768-1772], as Poland tried to expel Russian forces from the Commonwealth territory. The irregular and poorly commanded Polish forces suffered a major defeat at the hands of the regular Russian army. Adding to Poland's chaos were sporadic uprisings by bands of Ukrainian rebels called Haidamaky [Turkish word for marauders]. Formed as a result of extreme exploitation of the oppressed Ukrainian peasantry, the Haidamaky, in liaison with remaining Cossack bands, sporadically attacked Polish forces and its population.

The Left Bank autonomous Hetman State continued under Russian control. At the head of the state stood the hetman, elected theoretically by a general Cossack assembly, but in effect by senior officers who in turn were largely swayed by the tsar's preferences. The terms of autonomy were negotiated at each election of a new hetman, and this led over time to a steady erosion of his prerogatives. Nevertheless, the Hetmanate enjoyed a large measure of self-government, as well as considerable economic and cultural development. The Hetman State reached its peak when Ivan Mazepa became Hetman. Relying on the support of Russian Tsar Peter the Great, Mazepa exercised near monarchial powers in the Hetmanate. Urban life flourished and larger cities enjoyed municipal self-government. Literature, art and architecture in the distinctive Cossack style flourished under Mazepa's patronage, and the Kiev Mohyla Academy experienced its golden years. Nonetheless, the conditions of the peasantry worsened considerably over time.

Mazepa aspired to annex the Right Bank and create a united Ukrainian State. However, the centralizing reforms of Tsar Peter the Great appeared to threaten Ukraine's independence. In 1708, in furtherance of his plans for independence, Mazepa made a secret alliance with King Charles XII of Sweden. However, in a decisive Battle of Poltava [1709], their allied forces were soundly defeated. Mazepa fled to Moldova where he died shortly thereafter. Although Peter allowed the election of a successor to Mazepa, the Hetmanate autonomous prerogatives were severely curtailed.

In the meantime, in the very eastern part of Ukraine [today's Kharkiv region], Ukrainian peasants and some Cossacks, fleeing Polish rule, established non-serf settlements called Slobodas. Like the Hetmanate, Sloboda Ukraine enjoyed extensive internal autonomy.

In 1765, however, the autonomy of these settlements was abolished by Tsarina Catherine II. Furthermore, in 1775 she also ordered the Russia troops to destroy the Zaporozhian Sich, the bastion of Cossacks. Cossack leaders were exiled to Siberia and their lands were granted to Russian nobles. By the end of 1780, all regions, which were formerly under the Hetmanate, were incorporated into the Russian State. This essentially ended the Cossack period on the Left Bank.

After the Russians crushed the Polish uprising called the Confederacy of Bar in 1772, the great powers, Russia, Prussia and Austria, then decided to help themselves to Polish territory. Prussia took northern Poland, Austria took Ukraine's Halychyna [Galicia] and Russia took what is now eastern Belarus. In 1793, there was a second partition of Poland with Russia and Prussia taking more of Polish territory. The Poles rebelled in 1794, but they were crushed by the Prussians and Russians. Finally, in 1795 Prussia, Russia and Austria divided the last part of Poland between them. As a result, Austria received some additional, adjacent Ukrainian territory. This in effect ended Poland's rule of Ukrainian lands.

Period of Russian Tsarist and Austrian/Austro-Hungarian Rule [1795-1914]

As a result of the partitions of Poland [1772-1795], Ukraine became occupied by two empires, Russia and Austria. The western parts, Halychyna, Bukovyna and

Carpathian Ukraine, were incorporated into the Austrian [Habsburg] Empire. The rest of Ukraine, the central, southern and eastern parts, including Kiev, became part of Russia.

These two powers had strong central governments, mighty armies and powerful police ready to suppress any attempts by the Ukrainian population to gain self-determination.

Following the abolition of autonomy in the Hetmanate and Sloboda Ukraine, the Ukrainian lands in the Russian Empire formally lost all their distinctiveness. The territories were reorganized into regular Russian provinces administered by governors appointed from St Petersburg. As compensation for their lost rights as a ruling elite in the Hetmanate, the Cossack Starshyna were equalized with the Russian nobility. Many entered the imperial service and some achieved high government ranks. Through education, intermarriage and government service the Ukrainian nobility gradually became russianized, though many retained a sentimental attachment to the land and its folklore. Many literary works, although written in Russian, reflected Ukrainian customs, history and folklore. The most famous writer of such works was Mykola Hohol [Nikolai Gogol], author of "Taras Bulba". Folk stories, songs and art became very popular subjects in printed publications, which brought Ukrainian peasants and intelligentsia closer together. Clandestine societies, called Hromadas [communities], promoting Ukrainian culture were being organized. A secret political association, called the Brotherhood of Saints Cyril and Methodius [formed in 1826], propagated social equality and freedom of thought, conscience and speech. Schools, universities and theaters began to develop. Books and journals were written by university professors. Still, the majority of the books, although dealing with Ukrainian matters, were published in the Russian language until the appearance in 1840 of "Kobzar" [bard], a collection of poems by famous poet and painter Taras Shevchenko [1814-1861]. [See Appendix II - Testament: Poem by Taras Schevchenko]

Shevchenko, born a serf, was bought out of servitude by a group of artists who recognized his talent for painting, but he became famous mainly through his poems. In his poems Shevchenko protested against injustices and suppression of freedom in the Ukraine, encouraged preservation of Ukrainian language and reminded russianized descendents of Cossacks of the glory of Ukrainian past. His poetry reflected a conception of Ukraine as a free and democratic society. His works had a profound influence on the development of Ukrainian political thought. In 1847, Shevchenko was convicted for writing in the Ukrainian language, promoting independence of Ukraine and ridiculing members of the Russian Imperial House. He was exiled for ten years and forbidden to write. However, despite setbacks, Ukrainian opposition to Russian rule continued in the 1850's.

Agitation among the peasant class, coupled with the Russian defeat in the Crimean War [1853-1856], prompted

Tsar Alexander II to issue the Emancipation Manifesto in 1861 to grant freedom to the serfs of the Russian Empire. After the emancipation, however, the Ukrainian peasants were burdened by inadequate land allotments and heavy redemption payments that led to the impoverishment of many.

Toward the end of the 19th century, younger, primarily student-led Hromadas [communities] became involved in more overtly political activities with the goal of free and independent Ukraine. A movement for Ukrainian national and cultural revival began to gain momentum. The unrest that shook Russia in 1905 spawned worker strikes and peasant unrest in Ukraine as well. The consequent transformation of the tsarist autocracy into semi-constitutional monarchy led to some easing of Ukrainian national life.

The Ukrainian territories received by the Habsburg Austrian Empire in the partition of Poland experienced at first improved conditions. The Uniate Church was renamed the Greek Catholic Church and equalized in status with the Polish Roman Catholic Church. Educational reforms allowed for instructions in schools in the Ukrainian language. This led to the appearance, for the first time, of a large educated class within the Ukrainian population in Halychyna [Galicia]. However, on balance government policies favored the Poles. With time, the Polish nobility increased their influence on Austrian authorities and, by spreading rumors of Ukrainian sympathy to Russia, caused the replacement of Ukrainian by Polish language in state schools. Only private schools were allowed to use the Ukrainian language. Ukrainian literary figures were treated with animosity and suspicion by Austrian authorities. In 1845, to counter Polish ambition for independence, Austrian authorities began to lift restrictions on Ukrainian culture. Nonetheless, aspirations for independence of Ukrainians within the Austrian Empire were largely kept under control. Many changes came in 1848 as revolutions in Europe affected the circumstances within the Austrian Empire. Liberal reforms included end of censorship, a promise of a national constitution and end of serfdom in Halychyna. However, in the aftermath of the 1848 revolution, the imperial regime reached an accommodation with the Polish nobility that in effect ceded political control of Halychyna to the Poles. While in Russia Ukrainians were accused of siding with Poland, Polish activists convinced Austrian authorities of Ukrainian sympathy toward Russia. Faced with such situation, many Ukrainians started to think that maybe their only salvation was with Russia. They were called Russophiles.

But there were also many who remained steadfastly on pure Ukrainian ground, mainly energetic elements of the youth, but also some members of the old generation. They keenly absorbed the fiery poems of Taras Shevchenko and read other books of writers from eastern Ukraine, which was under Russian rule. A sense of national awakening began to develop among the Ukrainians, particularly in the eastern part of Halychyna. The years from 1860's to 1910's brought intensified political strife in western Ukraine. A nationalist movement was gaining strength and attracted more of the previously neutrally oriented people. As a result of all this political activity, Ukrainian national awareness and consciousness spread into wide masses of the population, which demanded greater autonomy for Halychyna. Their demands were not accepted outright, but over the course of the next several years a number of significant concessions were made toward the establishment of Halychyna's autonomy. In 1867, the Austrian Empire was reformed into a dualist Austro-Hungarian Empire. Six years later Halychyna became a de facto autonomous province of the empire, with Polish and to a lesser degree Ukrainian, as official languages. However, over time the Polish landowners gained political ascendancy in Halychyna. This shift in power to the Polish landowning class was not welcomed by the Ukrainians. Beginning in the 1880's, a mass emigration of the Ukrainian peasantry started to the United States, Canada and Brazil.

In 1899, overcoming differences and splits in the nationalistic movement, the Ukrainians formed the National Democratic Party. This party, founded by a distinguished historian Mykhailo Hrushevsky and a famous writer Ivan Franco, advocated Ukrainian independence. At the turn of the century the ethnic conflict in Halychyna intensified. Massive peasant strikes against the Polish landlords began in 1902. Ukrainian students engaged in continuous demonstrations and clashes with the Poles. In 1908, a student assassinated the Polish Halychyna governor.

By the outbreak of World War I, Ukrainians in Austrian Halychyna were still an overwhelmingly agrarian and politically disadvantaged society. Nevertheless, they had made impressive educational and cultural advances, possessed a large native intelligentsia and achieved a high level of national consciousness, all of which contrasted sharply with the prevailing situation in Russian ruled Ukraine.

Ukraine during World War I [1914-1918]

The First World War was a global war originating in Europe that lasted from July 1914 to November 1918. More than 70 million military personnel, including 60 million Europeans, were mobilized in one of the largest and costliest wars in history. Over nine million combatants and seven million civilians perished as a result of the war. The war drew in all the world's great powers assembled into two opposing alliances. The Allied Powers, consisting of the Russian Empire, the French Third Republic and the United Kingdom of Great Britain were pitted against the Central Powers of Germany and Austria-Hungary. These alliances reorganized and expanded as more nations entered the war. Italy, Japan and the United States joined the Allies, while the Ottoman Empire and Bulgaria joined the Central Powers.

The trigger for the war was the assassination of Archduke Franz Ferdinand of Austria, heir to the throne of Austria-Hungary, by Yugoslav nationalist Gavrilo Princip in Sarajevo on June 28, 1914. This set off a diplomatic crises when Austria-Hungary delivered an ultimatum to the King of Serbia and entangled alliances, formed over the previous decades, became involved. Within weeks the major powers were at war and the conflict soon spread around the world.

When the war broke out on July 28, 1914, Ukrainian Halychyna [Galicia] was part of the Austro-Hungarian Empire on the Central Powers side. The central and eastern parts of Ukraine, under Russian rule, were on the opposite, Allied Powers, side.

World War I was fought on mainly two fronts, the Western Front and the Eastern Front. Ukrainians served in both the Austro-Hungarian and Russian armies and were mostly involved on the Eastern Front, where Russia was fighting the Austro-Hungarian army supplemented with German units. About 3 million Ukrainians fought in Russia's armies and over 250,000 served in Austria's forces. The impact of the war on Ukrainians, who were caught between major adversaries in the conflict, was immediate and devastating. Some of the biggest battles on the Eastern Front occurred in Halychyna, and much of the western Ukraine suffered terribly from repeated offensives and occupations. Russian armies were initially successful and they occupied most of Halychyna.

The retreating Austrian authorities, suspecting the Ukrainians of pro-Russian sympathies, arrested, deported and executed hundreds without trial. Under Russian occupation the Ukrainians were also subjected to harsh treatment. Intent on russianizing the population, the tsarist authorities arrested and deported thousands of Ukrainian activists, shut down Ukrainian institutions and banned the use of Ukrainian language. They also launched a campaign to liquidate the Greek Catholic Church, exiling Metropolitan Andrei Sheptytsky to Russia in the process.

In late 1916 and into 1917, as a result of large casualties, dissatisfaction with the government's conduct of war grew in Russia. In March 1917, demonstrations in Petrograd culminated in the abdication of Tsar Nicholas II on March 15, 1917, and the appointment of a weak Provisional Government which shared power with the Petrograd Soviet Socialists. This arrangement led to confusion and chaos at the front and at home.

Taking advantage of the revolutionary situation, on March 17, 1917, representatives of various Ukrainian political, cultural and professional organizations gathered in Kiev and formed the Ukrainian Central Rada [Council]. In April, the more broadly convened Ukrainian National Council declared the Central Rada to be the highest national authority in Ukraine, and elected the historian Mykhailo Hrushevsky as its head. Although the Provisional Government recognized Ukraine's right to autonomy and the Central Rada as a legitimate representative body, there were unresolved disputes over its territorial jurisdiction and political prerogatives.

In Russia Vladimir Lenin, as the leader of the Bolshevik Party, gained popularity among the Russian population, and on November 7, 1917, the Russian Revolution brought him to power. Ukrainian-Russian relations deteriorated rapidly following the Bolshevik coup in Petrograd. The Central Rada refused to accept the new regime's authority over Ukraine, and on November 20, 1917 proclaimed the creation of the Ukrainian National Republic [UNR]. Soon after, the Central Rada took power in Kiev. In late December 1917, the Bolsheviks set up a rival Ukrainian People's Republic in the eastern city of Kharkiv. Hostilities against the UNR Central Rada government in Kiev began immediately. In turn, the Ukrainian National Republic declared independence on January 22, 1918 and broke ties with Russia. The Rada had limited armed forces at its disposal and was hard-pressed by the Kharkiv government which received Russian support. On February 9, 1918, the Bolshevik Red Guards entered Kiev, forcing the Central Rada to evacuate to Zhytomyr to the west. Faced with imminent defeat, the Rada turned to its hostile opponents, the Central Powers, for a truce and alliance which was accepted by Germany in return for desperately needed food supplies which Ukraine would provide to the Germans. As the Russian forces continued to retreat, the German and Austro-Hungarian armies drove the

Bolsheviks almost unopposed out of Ukraine, taking Kiev on March 1, 1918. Two days later, on March 3, the Russian Bolsheviks signed the Treaty of Brest-Litovsk, which formally ended hostilities on the Eastern Front of World War I and left Ukraine in the German sphere of influence. The treaty ceded Ukrainian lands west of the Kiev-Odessa line to the Central Powers of Germany and Austro-Hungary. Kiev remained under Russian rule.

However, disturbances continued across Ukraine as local Bolsheviks, peasant self-defense groups known as "Green Armies" and the anarchist Revolutionary Insurrection Army of Ukraine refused to subordinate to Germany.

On April 29, 1918, a former Imperial Army General Pavlo Skoropadsky led a successful German-backed coup against the Socialist-dominated Central Rada of Kiev. He proclaimed the conservative Ukrainian Hetmanate State and reversed many socialist policies of the former government.

Despite the limited success of the Central Powers on the Eastern Front, the outcome of the war was to be decided on the Western Front as the United States entered the war on the Allied side in April 1917 and the Allies rallied to drive back the Germans in a series of successful offensives. The successes forced the Austro-Hungarian Empire and Germany to agree to armistices with the Allied Powers on November 4 and 11, 1918, respectively. This in effect ended World War I with a victory for the Allied Powers. As a result, Germany and Austro-Hungary had to completely withdraw from Ukraine. Scoropadsky left Kiev with the Germans, and the Hetmanate was in turn overthrown by the Bolsheviks.

Ukraine in Aftermath of World War I [1918-1939]

Almost immediately after the defeat of Germany, Lenin's Bolshevik Russia government annulled the Brest-Litovsk Treaty and invaded Ukraine and other countries of eastern Europe that were formed under German protection. Simultaneously, the collapse of the Central Powers affected the former Austrian province of Halychyna, which was populated by Ukrainians and Poles. The Ukrainians proclaimed a Western Ukrainian National Republic in eastern Halychyna, which strived to unite with the Ukrainian National Republic [UNR] in eastern Ukraine. On the other hand, the Poles, who were mostly concentrated in western Halychyna, gave their allegiance to the newly formed Second Polish Republic. Both sides became increasingly hostile with each other. On January 18, 1919, the Paris Peace Conference granted eastern Halychyna to Poland for 25 years. Shortly thereafter, on January 22, 1919, the Western Ukrainian National Republic signed an Act of Union with the UNR in Kiev. By October 1919, the Western Ukrainian National Republic was defeated by the Polish forces in the Polish-Ukrainian War and eastern Halychyna was annexed to Poland.

In the meantime, the Ukrainian National Republic in Kiev under the direction of Symon Petlura faced imminent defeat in 1919 against the Bolsheviks. By 1920, all of central and eastern Ukraine, except Crimea, were in Bolshevik hands. Again facing imminent defeat, the UNR turned to its former adversary, Poland. In April 1920, Josef Pilsudsky of Poland and Simon Petlura of UNR signed a military agreement in Warsaw to fight the Bolsheviks. Just like the former alliance with Germany, this move sacrificed Ukrainian sovereignty, as Petlura recognized the Polish annexation of Halychyna. After initial successes of the UNR and Polish forces, the campaign developed into a stalemate. Petlura's forces, after several battles, were driven into Polish controlled territory. Faced with popular discontent at home, the Soviet Russia and Soviet Ukraine signed a peace treaty with Poland in March 1922 in Riga, Latvia. This effectively ended Poland's alliance obligations with Petlura's Ukrainian National Republic. According to the treaty, Soviet Russia recognized Polish control over western Ukraine, including Halychyna and western Volhynia. Poland, in turn, recognized central, eastern and southern areas of Ukraine as part of Soviet Ukraine. After its military and political defeat, the UNR continued to maintain control over some of its military forces and launched a series of guerilla raids into central Ukraine. But in November 1921, this force was surrounded by the Bolsheviks and destroyed.

On April 3, 1922, Joseph Stalin, a Bolshevik revolutionary during the Russian revolution of 1917, was appointed General

Secretary of the Central Committee of the Communist Party of the Soviet Union. The Communists, formerly Bolsheviks, proclaimed the Union of Soviet Socialists Republics [USSR]. On December 20, 1922, Ukraine was incorporated as the Ukrainian SSR into the USSR.

In the new State the Ukrainians initially enjoyed a relatively independent and prominent position. However, by 1928 Stalin had consolidated power in the Soviet Union and the Ukrainian Soviet Government became nearly powerless in the face of a centralized monolith Communist Party apparatus based in Moscow. Thus a campaign of cultural repression started, cresting in the 1930's when a massive famine ["Holodomor"] struck the Ukrainian Republic, claiming several millions of lives. Between 1934 and 1939, Stalin organized and led the "Great Purge", a massive campaign of repression of the government, armed forces and intelligentsia, in which millions of the so called "enemies of the working class" were imprisoned, exiled or executed often without due process.

Ukraine during World War II [1939-1945]

Despite strong pacifist sentiment after World War I, a nationalist movement developed in Germany unhappy with the significant territorial, colonial and financial losses incurred as a result of its defeat in the war. In 1933, Adolf Hitler became Chancellor of Germany and vowed to rectify the losses.

In August 1939, Nazi Germany under Hitler and the USSR under Stalin signed the Molotov-Ribbentrop Pact which secretly allied them to invade and partition Poland. Germany would get western Poland and the USSR would incorporate the Polish administrated Halychyna and Volhynia into the Ukrainian SSR.

World War II began on September 1, 1939, with the invasion of Poland by Nazi Germany and the subsequent declarations of war on Germany by France and United Kingdom on September 3. During September 1939, German forces occupied a major part of eastern Poland.

Eventually, World War II involved the vast majority of the world's nations forming two opposing military alliances, the Allies and the Axis.

Having invaded the eastern territories of Poland on November 1, 1939, USSR officially annexed the Western Ukraine territories and most of the Ukrainian nation was united into one country, the Ukrainian SSR. The Ukrainian population, particularly that of the western part of Ukraine, underwent a period of persecution by the Communist Ukrainian SSR regime. Many landowners and businesses lost their properties. People who did not join the Communist Party were considered suspicious, and many were imprisoned or deported to Siberia, as their loyalty to the new Communist government was questioned. Most of the resistance to the Soviet rule was provided by the Organization of Ukrainian Nationalists [OUN], which strived to achieve Ukrainian independence. The OUN was composed of two factions. The original, more moderate OUN, headed by Andriy Melnik, was referred to as OUN-M. The larger, more radical and younger group, OUN-B, was headed by Stepan Bandera. Both factions were ready to use any opportunity to free Ukraine from Russian domination.

In 1940, Stalin's invasion of Bukovina, currently southwestern Ukraine, violated their pact with Germany, as it went beyond their sphere of influence agreed with the Axis. Germany ended the pact when Hitler launched a massive invasion of the Soviet Union on June 22, 1941, in Operation Barbarossa. The primary targets of the surprise offensive were the Baltic region, Moscow and Ukraine. Hitler's objective was to eliminate the Soviet Union as a military power, exterminate Communism and guarantee access to the strategic resources needed to defeat Germany's remaining rivals.

As the Soviets retreated, thousands of political prisoners were executed by them in western Ukraine. When the German army entered Ukrainian territories, they were greeted by some Ukrainians as liberators. In Halychyna especially, there had long been a widespread belief that Germany, as the avowed enemy of Poland and the USSR, was Ukraine's natural ally for the attainment of their independence. On June 30, 1941, the Germans occupied Lviv. The organization of Ukrainian Nationalists [OUN-B] under the leadership of Stepan Bandera intended to take advantage of the retreat of Soviet forces and declared on the same day an independent Ukrainian State in Lviv. OUN-B thought they had found a new powerful ally in Nazi Germany to aid them in their struggle against the Soviet Union. The illusion was quickly shattered. Days after the invasion of Lviv, the leadership of the newly formed Ukrainian government, including Bandera, was arrested and sent to concentration camps in Germany.

As a result of the German crackdown on the OUN-B, the faction controlled by Melnyk [OUN-M] enjoyed advantage over its rival and was able to occupy some positions in the civil administration of former Soviet Ukraine during the first months of German occupation. However, alarmed by its growing strength in central and eastern Ukraine, the German Nazi authorities brutally cracked down on it, arresting and executing many of its members.

On August 20, 1941, Hitler appointed Erich Koch, a rabid anti-Ukrainian, as the Reichscommissar of Ukraine. Executions of thousands of Ukrainian nationalists followed. The Jewish population of Ukraine was also targeted through forced labor camps, executions and concentration camps. By the end of 1941, all of Ukraine was occupied by the Germans.

In 1942, during the Nazi occupation of Ukraine, an insurgent army UPA [Ukrayinska Povstanska Armiya] arose out of separate militant formations of the OUN. This partisan army engaged in a series of guerrilla actions against the Nazi occupiers.

The German offensive continued on Russian soil, and in August 1942 the Germans entered Stalingrad. Russia decided to make a stand at Stalingrad, and the battle for the city was on. Marked by fierce close quarters combat and direct assaults on civilians by air raids, it is often regarded as one of the single largest [nearly 2.2 million personnel] and bloodiest [1.7 - 2 million wounded, killed or captured] battles in the history of warfare. Bitter fighting in the city continued for about six months, and by February 1943 the Germans and their Axis allies were surrounded by the Russian army. Having exhausted their ammunition and food, the Germans were forced to surrender. After their victory at Stalingrad, the Russian army gained the initiative on the Eastern Front, and the Germans began their retreat. As the Soviet army occupied Ukraine from the retreating German army, many Ukrainian nationalists fearing retribution at the hands of the Communists fled to western countries including the United States, Canada, France and Great Britain. Those that stayed behind experienced interrogation, imprisonment and execution.

In 1944, the Western Allies invaded German-occupied France, while the Soviet Union regained all its territorial losses. The war in Europe concluded with the invasion of Germany by the Western Allies and the Soviet Union, and the subsequent German unconditional surrender on May 8, 1945.

World War II altered the political alignment and social structure of the world. The United Nations [UN] was established to foster international cooperation and prevent future conflicts. The United States and the Soviet Union emerged as rival superpowers, setting the stage for the Cold War which lasted for the next 46 years.

Ukraine after World War II [1945-1991]

After World War II the Ukrainian system of government was based on a one-party system ruled by the Communist Party of Ukraine, a part of the Communist Party of the Soviet Union [CPSU]. The Ukrainian Republic was one of the 15 constituent republics composing the Soviet Union. All of the political power and authority in the USSR was in the hands of Communist Party authorities, with little real power being concentrated in official bodies and organs. In such a system lower level authorities directly reported to higher level authorities and so on, with the bulk of the power being held at the highest echelons of the Communist Party.

When the war ended, the first task of the Soviet authorities under Stalin was to reestablish political control over the Ukrainian Republic, which had been entirely lost during the war. This was an immense task considering the widespread human and material losses. Ukraine lost a total of 5.5 million civilians and combatants. The material devastation was enormous. Hitler's orders to create a "zone of annihilation" in 1943, coupled with the Soviet military's scorched-earth policy, meant Ukraine lay in ruins. 80

percent of Kiev's city center was destroyed, as was most of the city center of the second largest city in Ukraine, Kharkiv. 19 million of Ukrainian people were left homeless after the war. The republic's industrial base, as so much else, was destroyed.

While the war brought to Ukraine enormous physical destruction, victory also led to territorial expansion. As a victor, the Soviet Union gained new prestige and land. The Ukrainian border was expanded to include some lands in Romania and Czechoslovakia which increased Ukraine's population by about 10 million.

After the war, the UPA Ukrainian nationalists fought guerrilla warfare against the Soviet Union until about 1950 in an attempt to gain full independence for Ukraine. It was particularly strong in the Carpathian Mountains and the entirety of Halychyna and Volhynia, all located in western Ukraine. Outside of West Ukraine, support of UPA was not significant, as the majority of the eastern Ukrainian population considered, and at times still view, OUN/UPA as not having taken a sufficiently strong anti-German stand during the war.

After the initial cleansing of the Ukrainian nationalist population, Ukraine, particularly the eastern part, became a very productive industrial base for the Soviet Union.

When Stalin died on March 5, 1953, the collective leadership of Khrushchev, Malenkov, Molotov and Beria took power and a period of de-Stalinization began. The

Central Committee of the Communist Party in Ukraine [CPU] openly criticized Stalin's russianization policies. On June 4, 1953, Oleksii Kyrychenko succeeded Leonid Melnikov as First Secretary of the CPU. This was significant since Kyrychenko was the first ethnic Ukrainian to lead the CPU since 1920's. In February 1954, Russia under Khrushchev, born in Russia close to the Ukrainian border, transferred Crimea as a gift to Ukraine from the Russian people; even if only 20 percent of the Crimean population was ethnic Ukrainian.

Significantly, the Ukrainian Republic became the center of Soviet arms industry and high-tech research. Ukraine was also turned into a Soviet military outpost during the cold war, a territory crowded by military bases packed with the most up-to-date weapon systems.

In October 1964, Khrushchev was deposed and succeeded by Leonid Brezhnev who was born in Ukraine. Brezhnev's rule was marked by social and economic stagnation. The new regime introduced the policy of uniting the different Soviet nationalities by merging the best elements of each nationality into the new one. This policy turned out to be, in fact, the reintroduction of the russianization policy. When Brezhnev died in 1982, he was succeeded by Yuri Andropov, who died shortly after taking power. Andropov was succeeded by Konstantin Chernenko who ruled for a little more than a year. Chernenko was then followed by Mikhail Gorbachev in 1985.

On April 26, 1986, the town of Pripyat in northern Ukraine was the site of the Chernobyl disaster when a nuclear power plant exploded. The fallout contaminated large areas of northern Ukraine and parts of Belarus.

By the time Gorbachev came to power, Russia was in severe economic stagnation and political disorder. Recognizing this, Gorbachev introduced a two-tiered policy of reform. On one level, he initiated a policy of "Glasnost", or freedom of speech. On the other level, he began a program of economic reform known as "Perestroika", or rebuilding. By giving people complete freedom of expression, he unwittingly unleashed emotions and political feelings that had pent up for decades, and which proved to be extremely powerful when brought out into the open.

Demonstrations and rebellions in the Soviet Republics demanding independence followed. On August 24, 1991, the Ukrainian Parliament adopted the Act of Declaration of Independence of Ukraine. The Act established Ukraine as an independent state.

As other Soviet Republics declared independence, on December 26, 1991, the Soviet Union was dissolved.

Ukraine since Independence [1991-Present]

After the dissolution of the Soviet Union and Ukraine's independence in 1991, Ukraine under the presidencies of both Leonid Kravchuk and Leonid Kuchma maintained cautious but good relations with Russia for 14 years. Both were members of the Communist Party and held high political offices in the pre-independence Ukraine SSR. Kravchuk was a transitional figure with little influence on Ukraine's future events. Kuchma who followed him as president in 1994 served as Prime Minister under Kravchuk between October 1992 and September 1993. Kuchma came from the Chernihiv region of Ukraine, about 50 miles north of Kiev and close to the Ukrainian border with Russia. He had a successful career in the Soviet machine-building industry, having been involved in the design and development of space rockets. Later in his career he was the technical director of the Baikonur launch complex in Kazakhstan. Most of his support came from Ukraine's industrial area in the east and south. His presidency was surrounded by numerous corruption scandals and lessening of media freedoms. Opponents accused Kuchma of being involved in 2000 in the killing of journalist Georgiy Gongadze, which he has always denied. In 2001, an Ukrainian district court ordered prosecutors to drop criminal charges against him on grounds of insufficient evidence. Rumors persisted that the immunity from prosecution was granted in return for his graceful departure from office in 2005. His foreign policy was contradictory, as he signed a Treaty of Friendship, Cooperation and Partnership with Russia, but on the other hand, advocated Ukraine's membership in the European Union [EU], and signed a special partnership agreement with NATO. During his presidency Ukraine became a non-nuclear nation, when in June 1, 1996, it sent the last of its 1900 nuclear warheads it had inherited from the Soviet Union to Russia for dismantling. He also oversaw the development of Ukraine's first post-Communist constitution which was adapted in 1996. Although after the election he appointed a team of reformists to develop a program of economic reform, progress was slow and resulted in only a modest improvement of the economy.

In December 1999, Kuchma unexpectedly nominated Victor Yushchenko to be the prime minister. Ukraine's economy showed improvement during Yushchenko's cabinet service. However, his government, particularly Deputy Prime Minister Yulia Timoshenko, soon became embroiled in a confrontation with influential leaders of the coal mining and natural gas industries. The conflict resulted in a no-confidence vote by the parliament, orchestrated by the Communists who opposed Yushchenko's economic policies and by the country's powerful oligarchs. Hence in 2001, Yushchenko was removed from office and Victor Yanukovych became the new Prime Minister. In 2004, Leonid Kuchma announced he would not run for reelection.

Two major candidates emerged in the 2004 presidential election. Victor Yanukovych, the incumbent Prime Minister supported by both Kuchma and Russia, advocated closer ties with Russia. The main opposition candidate, Victor Yushchenko, wanted Ukraine to turn its attention westward and eventually join the EU. The campaign between the two candidates was bitter and violent. In September 2004, Yushchenko became seriously ill due to dioxin poisoning resulting in a greatly disfigured face. Yushchenko claimed he was poisoned by government agents. Future investigations of how and who perpetrated the poisoning were inconclusive.

In the runoff election Yanukovych officially won by a narrow margin, but Yushchenko and his supporters alleged that vote rigging and intimidation cost him many votes, especially in eastern Ukraine. In the immediate aftermath of the run-off vote, a series of massive protests and political events took place in Ukraine from late November 2004 to January 2005. Kiev, the Ukrainian capital, was the focal point of the movement's campaign of civil resistance, with thousands of protestors demonstrating daily on the Independence Square [Maidan]. Nationwide the democratic protests, called the Orange Revolution, were highlighted by a series of acts of civil disobedience, sit-ins and general strikes organized by the revolution. The nationwide protest succeeded when the results of the original run-off were annulled, and a revote was ordered by Ukraine's Supreme Court for December 26, 2004. Under intense scrutiny by domestic and international observers, the second run-off showed Yushchenko the winner with 52 percent of the vote. Yanukovych resigned from office, and his cabinet was dismissed on January 5, 2005.

Prior to entering politics, Yushchenko had a long career in banking. In 1993, he was appointed Chairman of the National Bank of Ukraine [Ukraine's Central Bank]. As a central banker, Yushchenko played an important part in the creation of Ukraine's national currency, the Hryvnia, and the establishment of a modern regulatory system for commercial banking. In 2002, Yushchenko became the leader of the Our Ukraine political coalition, which received a plurality of seats in the year's parliamentary elections.

Yushchenko's first year in office was turbulent and marked by numerous dismissals and appointments at all levels. He appointed Yulia Timoshenko as Prime Minister and Petro Poroshenko as Secretary of the Security and Defense Council. In the summer of 2005, according to former Security Service of Ukraine Chairman Oleksander Tyrchynov, Yushchenko prevented an investigation into alleged fraudulent practices in the transport of Turkmen natural gas to Ukraine and the arrest of Yuri Boyko for abuse of office while heading Naftogas. Later that year he was accused of having his election campaign financed by a Russian tycoon, which he strongly denied. Financing of election campaigns by foreign citizens is illegal in Ukraine. On September 9, 2005, Yushchenko fired his government led by Yulia Timoshenko, after resignations and claims of corruption. As a result of these disorderly events during his administration, Yushchenko's popularity declined sharply. In the parliamentary elections of March 2006, the Our Ukraine party received less than 14 percent of the national vote.

In August 2006, Yushchenko appointed his onetime opponent in the presidential race, Victor Yanukovych, to be the new Prime Minister. This was generally regarded as an attempt to improve relations with Russia. On April 2,

2007, Yushchenko signed an order to dissolve parliament and call early elections. The opposition claimed this was illegal under the Ukrainian Constitution and referred the case to the Constitutional Court for resolution. In May 2007, Yushchenko illegally dismissed three members of Ukraine's Constitutional Court, thus preventing the court from ruling on the constitutionality of his decree. In a poll conducted in 2007 the majority of Ukrainians polled indicated that they distrusted Yushchenko.

Despite the poor poll results, on November 10, 2009, Victor Yushchenko was nominated for a second term as President. His opponents, in the election scheduled for January 17, 2010, were Tymoshenko and Yanukovych. In the first round of elections he received only 5.45 percent of the vote, the worst result for any sitting President in the history of Ukraine. In the run-off that followed Yanukovych was victorious over Timoshenko and became the 4th Ukrainian President.

His election was welcomed by Russia, and Patriarch Krill of the Moscow Orthodox Church attended his inauguration on February 20, 2010. Yanukovych came from the eastern region of Ukraine [Donetsk Oblast]. He was twice the Prime Minister and leader of the Party of Regions.

His stated policy was to maintain a balanced position of cooperation with both Russia and EU. He did not support Ukraine's entry into NATO, claiming that he did not intend to join any military bloc. However, during the course of his presidency he appeared to favor a closer relationship with Russia. To improve the lives of the working class Yanukovych increased social benefits and raised pensions.

After the 2010 presidential elections, a number of criminal cases were brought against Yulia Tymoshenko. On October 11, 2011, she was convicted of embezzlement and abuse of power. She was sentenced to seven years in prison and ordered to pay the State $188 million. The prosecution and conviction were viewed as politically biased by many governments, most prominently the EU and the United States.

On April 21, 2010, in Kharkiv, Yanukovych and Dmitry Medvedev, the Russian President, signed the 2010 Ukrainian-Russian Naval Base for Natural Gas Treaty, whereby the Russian lease on naval facilities in Crimea would be extended beyond 2017 by 25 years with an additional 5-year renewal option in exchange for a multi-year discounted contract to provide Ukraine with Russian gas.

Yanukovych had been widely criticized for extensive corruption and cronyism. More than half of his ministers appointed by him were either born in the eastern Donbas region or made some crucial part of their careers there. Almost half of the budget for social and economic development was allotted to the Donbas region.

In November 2013, a series of events transpired that eventually led to Yanukovych's ouster as President. Yanukovych refused to comply with an EU demand to release former Prime Minister Tymoshenko from prison. Furthermore, he rejected a pending EU association agreement, favored by the majority of Ukrainians, and instead chose to pursue a Russian loan bailout and closer ties with Russia. This led to massive protests and the occupation of Kiev's Independence Square [Maidan] by young pro-European Ukrainians. The protests continued without interruption and were dubbed the "Euromaidan". Ukrainians from the western regions arrived by bus and train to join the protesters. Priests led daily prayers at the barricades, and a chapel in the middle of the square provided daily mass and counseling.

On January 2014, deadly clashes developed in Independence Square and in other areas of Ukraine, as Ukrainian citizens confronted the Berkut and other special police units. In February, the violent clashes between protesters and special police forces led to many deaths and injuries and Ukraine appeared to be on the brink of civil war. Fighters of the Right Sector ultra-nationalist movement and the national party Svoboda were especially the most organized and effective of the Euromaidan forces battling the police.

On February 21, 2014, Yanukovych claimed that, after lengthy discussions, he had reached an agreement with the opposition. Later that day, however, he fled the capital for

Kharkiv and eventually to exile in southern Russia. On February 22, the Ukrainian Parliament voted to remove him from his post, on the grounds that he was unable to fulfill his duties. On February 23, Oleksandr Turchynov was designated as acting President of Ukraine. On the same day, pro-Russian demonstrations against the turn of events in Ukraine broke out in Simferopol, the capital of Crimea, and Sevastopol. Masked gunmen, believed to be ethnic Russian extremists, took over several government buildings and raised the Russian flag. On February 27, masked Russian troops without insignia took over the Supreme Council [Parliament] of Crimea, and captured strategic sites across Crimea. On the same day, Sergey Aksyonov was elected as the pro-Russian Prime Minister. In a referendum held on March 16, 2014, over 90 percent of voters in Crimea chose to secede from Ukraine. On March 18, Crimea was annexed by Russia. Ukraine considers the annexation illegal and a violation of international law. Russia was suspended from the G8 group of nations and sanctions were imposed on Russia by the U.S. and EU. In addition, U.S. President Barak Obama adopted a policy of political isolation of Russia in the international arena.

After the annexation of Crimea, Russia continued to deploy troops on the southern and eastern borders of Ukraine, areas that are dominated by ethnic Russians. By the end of March, there were as many as 40,000 Russian troops stationed on the border. In early April, pro-Russian protesters and armed militants took over several government buildings and police stations in Donetsk and Luhansk, as well as other towns in the Donbas region. The government of Kiev responded with military force and employed local militias to help push back the separatists.

In April 2014, the leaders of the separatists Alexander Zakharchenko and Igor Plotnitsky established, respectively, the Donetsk People's Republic [DPR] and the Luhansk People's Republic [LPR]. A referendum on regional autonomy held in Donetsk and Luhansk, on May 11, showed that over 90 percent of the voters favored self-rule. No international observers monitored the vote and the Ukrainian government denounced the referendum as illegal.

In the midst of the crises, the Ukrainian people elected Petro Poroshenko as their 5th President on May 25, 2014. Poroshenko held several high-level positions in previous governments and has long supported the country's pro-European movement.

In July and August 2014, the Ukrainian armed forces successfully dislodged the separatist militants from some of their strongholds and began to move on the key cities of Donetsk and Luhansk. It was during this time that a Malaysia Airlines Boeing 777 crashed in eastern Ukraine near the Russian border on July 17, killing all 298 passengers and crew members. A lengthy investigation concluded that the plane was probably downed by separatist forces using a Russian-supplied Buk missile.

In August 2015, Russia's President Putin stepped up his support of the separatists by deploying some Russian troops to fight in Ukraine and by supplying them with military equipment including tanks, armored personnel carriers, artillery and surface-to-air-missiles. Fighting a heavily supplied separatist force, joined by Russian troops, Ukrainian forces lost ground and suffered heavy casualties. Fearing further casualties and loss of more territory, Ukraine agreed to a ceasefire plan during talks with separatist representatives, Russian officials and several European leaders in Minsk, Belarus, on September 5, 2014. The plan [Minks-1] called for a cease-fire along lines of control, an exchange of prisoners, monitoring of the cease-fire by the Organization for Security and Cooperation in Europe [OSCE] and withdrawal of illegal armed groups from the territory of Ukraine. The signing of the agreement led to the end of the Russian-supported offensive against the Ukrainian forces, but did not fully end the fighting. Nor were any of the provisions of the agreement fully implemented. While actively engaged with allies in Europe in seeking a resolution of the crisis, the U.S. administration had, for the most part, left the leading role in negotiating a settlement to Germany, France and Ukraine, whose representatives met with those of Russia in the so-called Normandy format, named after the region where the meeting first occurred.

Early in 2015, heavier fighting between separatists and Ukrainian government forces flared-up again. Recognizing the failure of the Minks-1 pact to end the conflict, the presidents of France [Hollande], Russia [Putin], Ukraine [Poroshenko] and Chancellor Merkel of Germany met again in Minsk in early February 2015 to try to secure a new agreement to stop the fighting. On February 12, a new cease-fire agreement, Minks-2, was signed by the participants.

Under Minks-2 the ceasefire was to be monitored by the OSCE. The agreement called for local elections in the rebel-held regions and, more importantly and controversially for Kiev, for legal and constitutional reforms to be negotiated with the rebels to give a special "decentralized" status to the region, as well as amnesty for the separatist leaders. The elections and reforms were to be implemented before the end of 2015. The return of control to Ukraine of its side of the Russia-Ukraine border was conditioned on the implementation of the decentralization reforms.

Although there were some lulls in the fighting since February 2015, a total bilateral case-fire has not materialized. The cease-fire violations continue to result in numerous civilian, Ukrainian military and separatist casualties, estimated at close to 10,000 dead since 2015. As of the middle of 2017, the Minks-2 agreement has not been fully implemented by either side, despite commitments to do so.

Both the United States and the EU made the full implementation of the Minks-2 protocol a precondition to easing sanctions on Russia. However, President Poroshenko does not have the necessary votes in the Rada to pass an amendment to the constitution to grant the increased autonomy for Donbas called for in the Minks-2 agreement.

On March 15, 2017, bending to the pressure of right-wing nationalists, Ukraine ordered the imposition of a trade blockade on the eastern Donbas region controlled by the separatists. Responding to the blockade, the Russian-backed separatists assumed control over some 40 enterprises owned by Ukrainian interests to ensure payment of their taxes locally and not to Kiev. These actions by both sides to the conflict further undermined the ability to fully implement the Minks-2 agreement.

The unresolved conflict in Donbas and the slow implementation of reforms has resulted in a growing Ukraine fatigue in Europe. Also, the level of support by the new U.S. Administration is unknown.

What Went Wrong?

On January 22, 1990, on Ukraine Unity Day, in a forerunner to Ukraine's independence, some 3 million Ukrainians joined hand-to-hand in a human chain between Kiev and Lviv to commemorate the January 22, 1919, union of the Ukrainian National Republic with the Western Ukrainian National Republic to form a short-lived state. A year-and-a-half later on August 24, 1991, Ukraine became a fully independent state. Euphoria reigned across Ukraine and distant lands where many Ukrainian expatriates live. Ukrainians around the world were united in celebrating this glorious moment in their history. Ukraine was in bloom again.

Twenty-five years later, Ukrainians are confronting each other on front lines in East Ukraine, members of the parliament occasionally engage in brawls, corruption is widespread, the economy is stagnant, lives of average Ukrainians is dismal, separatist occupy parts of eastern Ukraine and Crimea is not part of Ukraine anymore.

What went wrong?

After the initial euphoria over independent Ukraine subsided, the country was faced with a multitude of social, economic, political and foreign policy issues.

For the first 15 years after independence, the government of Ukraine was in the hands of transitional figures, Kravchuk and Kuchma, who still had the mentality of the Soviet days. They concentrated on running the essential services of the government with emphasis on political organization and economy. Little effort was made to unify the country, despite obvious social and ethnic differences across the regions. At the same time, they saw an opportunity to enrich themselves with both stature and wealth. A weak justice system and a non-transparent government combined with business-political ties allowed corruption to flourish from top to bottom.

The transition period set the stage for what was to follow. A political elite started to emerge, forming often non-transparent alliances between different parties and business groups to improve their governmental power. This political and business elite, often acting in concert, began to compete with each other for leadership of the country. Victor Yanukovych, Victor Yushchenko and Yulia Timoshchenko emerged as the key politicians. Unable to unify the country or substantially improve the economy, they played "musical chairs", and took turns at leading the country. Promises of EU membership or better relations with Russia were mostly meant to gain political support from certain segments of the population. In endless speeches in the parliament politicians from an array of political parties pledged a better future for all Ukrainians, while ignoring the growing dissatisfaction across the country. The people elected them, but the business elite, the oligarchs, controlled them.

When independence came in 1991, the Ukrainian people had been under continuous Soviet domination for almost 50 years, as part of the Ukraine SSR. Even though they were delighted and proud to be free Ukrainians, they found adjusting to the new situation difficult, akin to being in a deep slumber for many years and suddenly waking up and facing a world they were not familiar with. Trying to figure out what direction the country should take was difficult and also divisive for both the leaders and the people of Ukraine. As a dialogue began between different factions of the population as to the course Ukraine should take with regard to foreign policy, the divisions among Ukrainians that persisted to a great extent throughout its history began to surface. The majority of people in the central regions of Ukraine, including Kiev, preferred a neutral approach to foreign policy. However, they thought that joining the EU would be beneficial for Ukraine for political and economic reasons. Most were not in favor of joining the North Atlantic Treaty Organization [NATO]. They wanted the government to concentrate on improving the economy and eliminate corruption. The people of western Ukraine advocated joining the EU to be politically closer to the West. Many of the westerners were in favor of joining NATO to provide a buffer against a potential encroachment from Russia in the future. They had bad memories from the days of the Soviet rule and wanted to break ties with Russia faster than was possible. They accused the eastern and southern regions of Ukraine of being too friendly towards Russia, considering that many Ukrainians in the past were persecuted, jailed and executed by the Soviet regime. The people of the eastern and southern parts of Ukraine, in turn, advocated closer ties with Russia. Many spoke Russian and some had relatives living across the border in western Russia. They also accused the people of western Ukraine of collaboration with Nazi Germany during World War II that brought great suffering to their people. Some of the older generation had served in the Soviet army fighting the Germans.

As the elected government and politicians failed to unite the country and engaged in contradictory statements and policies with regard to closer association with the West [EU, U.S., NATO] or Russia, radical groups, on both sides, advocating violence to have their way started to surface in Ukraine. Peaceful protests by Ukrainians during the Orange Revolution in 2004 and the Euromaidan Revolution in 2013-2014 were infiltrated by these groups, and turned violent. Some of these groups may have been instigated and supported by foreign operatives.

After Ukraine's independence, Russian political and economic influence over Ukraine remained strong with Moscow determined to ensure that despite any changes in the government in Kiev, Ukraine would remain on good terms with Russia. Occupying a sensitive position between Russia and the NATO member states of Poland, Slovakia, Hungary and Romania, Ukraine became to play a prominent role in the geopolitical competition between the West and Russia. Ethnic Russians make up about 18 percent of Ukraine's population and are concentrated in the eastern and southern parts of the country. They form a majority in Crimea with 60 percent of the population. In addition, Ukrainians in the east and south also tend to be Russian-speaking. They are generally suspicious of Ukrainian nationalism and support closer ties with Russia. The collapse of the Yanukovych government after the Euromaidan revolution did not sit well in Moscow. Russia under President Vladimir Putin reacted with great hostility toward the events in Kiev, referring to them as an illegal coup. Russia responded to the change of government in Kiev by sizing Ukraine's Crimea region and annexing it on March 18, 2014. In April 2014, armed pro-Russian separatists supported by Moscow sized parts of the Donbas region of eastern Ukraine and the fighting between them and Ukrainian Armed Forces continues until today, despite a Minks-2 peace agreement to end the fighting signed by both parties.

In response to the Russian annexation and the conflict in the Donbas region, both the United States and the European Union initiated a series of sanctions against Russia. The EU has shown readiness to assist in the settlement of the conflict and has been instrumental in providing a coordinating role in the development of the Minks-2 pact. It is strongly opposed to providing Ukraine with offensive weapons to avoid further inflaming the conflict on its borders. The U.S.

maintains a firmer stand against the separatists, as well as Russia. It accuses Russia of supplying the separatists with both manpower and weapons. Some hawks in Congress have even urged the U.S. administration to supply the Ukrainian military forces with offensive weapons.

At the beginning of 2015 Ukraine's economy took a sharp downturn. As a result the International Monetary Fund [IMF] agreed to pump $17.5 billion into Ukraine's economy in a four year bailout, releasing the funds in installments subject to the government'a progress on economic and anti-corruption reforms. As of 2017, Ukraine has received $7.62 billion in the program. But the price of that help came in the form of higher energy bills and wage freezes. With the help of the IMF loan, Ukraine's economy improved from a sharp recession to a slow growth. A growth rate of about 2 percent is projected for 2017. Investments are down because of the conflict in the east of the country and the middle class is impoverished.

Hence, after 25 years of independence, the health of the Ukrainian nation is clouded in uncertainty. The people who were entrusted to lead independent Ukraine failed to build Ukraine's institutions and unify the country. Instead they build their own fortunes. There is a frozen conflict with separatists in the east, the justice system is politicized, the people are frustrated with the slow pace of reforms and the economy faces an uncertain future. Joining the EU in not on the agenda anymore.

Will Ukraine Bloom Again?

Today Ukraine is a divided country trying to find the right course forward amid domestic turmoil and international pressures. Much has been accomplished to establish a free and independent state, however, much remains to finish the job. The main hindrance to further progress toward building a stronger nation is Ukraine's disunity, aggrevated by foreign political forces. In fact, this obstacle has become the key to the question: "Will Ukraine bloom again?"

Ukraine's location as a buffer state between the EU/NATO countries and Russia makes political influence over Ukraine a strategic objective of these world powers. Their political pressures pose a continuous threat to Ukraine's ability to act in its own interest. Ukraine has become a political football that's being kicked around by players of opposing countries trying to score a goal in their favor.

Ukraine must reject the political pressures forced on them by the foreign powers, heal the many wounds opened among the Ukrainian people in the course of its history and chart its own independent course for the full benefit of its people.

Ukraine needs leaders who put priority on uniting its people to create a modern and vibrant democratic state for all Ukrainians, including the separatists. Only a united people who feel a strong allegiance to their country are going to work on the country's behalf.

The current Ukrainian government of President Poroshenko and Prime Minister Groysman has taken a one-track foreign policy approach by trying to fully align itself politically with the West and refusing to negotiate directly with the separatists. They assume that the U.S. and EU will provide them effectively with permanent protection against Russia and eventually force Russia to abandon their support for the separatists in exchange for lifting of western imposed sanctions. This is "wishful thinking" and does not reflect reality. The western countries have their own priorities and Ukraine is only one of the many global issues they have to deal with. Any actions they take with regard to Ukraine will only reflect their own national security interests.

Russia is a strong world military power and under Putin's leadership has shown the ability to resist international pressure. Western sanctions against Russia, while hurting it economically, have not deterred Russia from supporting the separatists. If the West, particularly the United States, were to provide offensive weapons to Ukraine to bolster their military strength, Russia could easily match this by supplying more weapons to the separatists. This would only result in a wider conflict with additional Ukrainian casualties on both sides.

It's been more than two years now since the Minks-2 agreement entered into force. Except for occasional periods of ceasefire, nothing else has been accomplished to implement some of the other key provisions of the pact, including elections, constitutional reforms, decentralization, amnesty, humanitarian aid and return of Ukainian borders to Kiev's control. This is to be expected, since Minks-2 only lays out a path toward a political settlement of the conflict. Extensive negotiations must follow to come to an agreement on each provision of the pact before implementation can begin, as both sides have different interpretations regarding the key elements of Minks-2. In addition, the provisions of the pact, imposed on President Poroshenko by a Russian-supported separatists offensive in 2015, are considered to be unfavorable to Ukraine by its Parliament, where support for their implementation is questionable.

Nonetheless, at some point, the Ukrainian Government and Parliament must be prepared to resolve the Donbas impasse by direct negotiations with the separatists to resolve the differences in the interpretation of the agreement. By refusing to negotiate with them, the Ukrainian government is only pushing the separatists into Putin's lap. Negotiations in good faith by both sides is the best way to bring the Donbas conflict to an end.

The first issue they need to resolve should be how to define Ukraine's new political structure. Ukraine must be prepared to decentralize some of its powers to all its regions. The regions should receive greater control over taxation and spending as well as the ability to directly elect their own governors. The regions should be allowed to have their own police force and National Guard. Social issues such as education, language and culture should also be under their control. From Moscow's perspective, a significant amount of devolution allows Putin to assert that he has successfully protected the rights of Ukraine's ethnic Russian or Russian-oriented citizens who live in the east and south of the country. From Kiev's point of view, meanwhile, divisive issues as the status of the Russian language or the politics of historical memory get decided at the local level, where they belong. This will allow a common civic identity to develop around Ukraine's rich multicultural makeup.

Next, Russia must explicitly acknowledge Ukraine's right to seek membership in the EU as well as any non-military political or economic relationship with Brussels it may choose instead. Most Ukrainians now favor eventual EU membership, and the country has already signed an Association Agreement with the EU. Russia must accept the fact that Ukraine is determined to pivot toward Europe politically and economically. Following a period of reconciliation, a referendum on Ukraine's membership in the EU should be put to a vote. It may take several years for Ukraine to join the EU, giving it some time to rebuild relations with Russia.

In exchange for Russia agreeing to Ukraine's EU membership, Ukraine, in turn, should agree not to seek NATO membership. The reality is that many NATO countries would not support Ukraine's membership anyway. Furthermore, NATO membership remains divisive within Ukraine. Recent polls indicate that a plurality of Ukrainians do not favor NATO membership. Kiev's pusuit of NATO membership would undermine its goal to overcome its regional differences. Although some might criticize Ukraine's agreement to forgo NATO membership as appeasement, others may see it as a realistic step that costs Ukraine little, while potentially strengthening its hand on other issues much more fundamental to its future.

The Crimea issue is least subject to compromise. Crimea has a majority ethnic Russian population. In addition, a large Russian naval base, vital to its national security, is located on the peninsula. It is highly unlikely that Russia will return Crimea to Ukraine. Hence, it would be best to defer the Crimea negotiations until some later time, when relations between Ukraine and Russia are normalized. Perhaps some form of payment to Ukraine for Crimea might be possible or an agreement could be reached to return Crimea at some future time.

Ukrainians are highly patriotic people and they care much about their country's direction. They demonstrated this abundantly during the Euromaidan protests. They were the engine of the revolution, but in the end the steering wheel appears to be in the hands of leaders and politicians who are steering their own independent course. Some of them even masquarade as ethnic Ukrainians, electing not to reveal their true ancestry. It only follows that President Poroshenko's approval rating is less than 20 percent. Most Ukrainians, regardless from which region they come, disapprove of his administration's handling of the Donbas conflict, government reforms and economy.

Young Ukrainians played important roles in the protest movements of 2004 and 2014. If these young people can institutionalize their participation in the country's political process, they could provide Ukraine with new leadership which it badly needs. In early July 2016, a new push to form a liberal political party was reportedly launched by many young, former Maidan activists who are now in the government, Paliament or civil society. The new movement backs free-market approaches and specifically supports the small- and medium-sized business community. The group is a staunch proponent of tough anti-corruption measures and a professional, impartial judiciary. The group intends to rely on social media, civic networks and crowd funding to spread its message and build support. If this movement can evolve into a full-fledged political party, it could present a challenge to the Poroshenko Bloc Party. Hence, potentially, young and highly patriotic leaders may emerge in the presidential and parliamentary elections scheduled for 2019, and they may well become symbols around which Ukrainians could rally. They could also conceivably bring to the table a new approach to the settlement of the Donbas conflict.

A dark horse in the next election may be Nadia Savchenko, a former Lieutenant in the Ukrainian Ground Forces and an unaffiliated member of the Parliament. Released from a Russian prison in May 2016, in a prisoner exchange, she is viewed in Ukraine as a national hero and a possible political leader. Many of Savchenko's supporters are from rural parts of Ukraine, attracted by her nationalistic views and the crude verbal attacks she has launched against the governing elite. She has become a mouthpiece for the anger many simple people have for Ukraine's political leaders. Since her release from Russian prison, she has traveled back and forth aross Ukraine, visiting steelworkers, farmers and soldiers on the front lines in Donbas. On several occasions Savchenko has stated that she is prepared to become President of Ukraine if the Ukrainians wish so. She has shown some flexibility by meeting with the Donbas separatists in an attempt to arrange a prisoner exchange. Her meetings for that purpose were received negatively by the government, which refuses to meet directly with the separatists.

Ukraine is a relatively small country. It's negative birth rate will reduce its population to only 40 million by 2025. Ukraine is also getting older. It's 65+ population in 2025 will increase to about 20 percent from the current 16.5 percent. It's military is no match against Russia. Military intervention on their behalf by either EU or U.S. is highly unlikely.

Realistically, to avoid a frozen conflict in the east of their country, Ukraine needs to negotiate a settlement with the Donbas separatists. At some point, hopefully soon, they need to meet half-way and find a peaceful solution. The sooner it comes, the better it will be for the Ukrainian people. Ukraine needs more time to implement political, economic and judicial reforms to strengthen its ability to govern. A peaceful environment will go a long way to accomplish this goal.

Once the geopolitical issues are resolved and the threat of wider hostilities is removed, it will become possible for the Russian-Ukrainian economic relationship to improve. Even with the current conflict between them, Russia is still Ukraine's largest trading partner. End of hostilities would also increase the level of domestic and foreign investments in Ukraine's economy.

It would be unwise to underestimate the complexity of the current dilemma facing Ukraine. Tough decisions and painful compromises lie ahead.

Nevertheless, knowing the Ukrainian people's ability to persevere under difficult circumstances, the author is confident that in the end Ukraine will develop strong leadership, make the right decisions, overcome its remaning obstacles and bloom again.

APPENDIX I

National Opera House
Kiev, Ukraine

Cathedral of St. Sophia
Kiev, Ukraine

Khreschatyk Street
Kiev, Ukraine

Khreschatyk Street
Kiev, Ukraine

Independence Square-Maidan
Kiev, Ukraine

Taras Shevchenko National University
Kiev, Ukraine

APPENDIX II

TESTAMENT

ZAPOVIT
Poem by Taras Shevchenko
December 25, 1845

When I die, bury me
In a grave
Amid the wide steppe
Of my beloved Ukraine
So that the wide plains
The Dnieper's steep shore
My eyes can see, my ears can hear
The mighty river roar

When from Ukraine it flows
Into the blue sea
Loud with the blood of foes
I will leave it all and fly
To God himself
And I will pray
But till that day
I don't know God

Oh bury me, then rise up
And break your chains
Then with the tyrants blood
Water the freedom you have gained
And in the mighty family
Of all men free
Maybe sometime with kind, soft words
You will also remember me

Translated by Stephan A Dzerovych
May 2017

SOURCES

www.wikipedia.org
www.britannica.com
www.infoplease.com
www.globalissues.com
www.focus-economics.com
www.bbc.com
www.pbs.org
www.census.com
www.unian.info
www.ukraine-insight.com
www.nytimes.com
www.kyivpost.com
www.tradingeconomics.com
www.theguardian.com
www.d-maps.com>europe>ukraine

ABOUT THE AUTHOR

The author has worked as an electronics engineer for the U.S. Navy in the Field of Anti-Submarine Warfare [ASW] for forty years [1957-1997]. As Head of the Intelligence Branch of the Naval Applied Science Laboratory in New York City, he had responsibility for development of intelligence systems related to the Navy's ASW programs. Later in his career, the author worked as the Head of the Sonar Development Branch of the Naval Undersea Warfare Center in New London, Connecticut and Newport, Rhode Island. His responsibilities included the conduct of programs in the areas of submarine sonar and ocean surveillance.

During his career, the author participated on numerous panels and committees related to acoustic intelligence and sonar systems. In addition, he provided consultations and recommendations on intelligence and technical matters to the Chief of Naval Operations and Naval Sea Systems Command in Washington D.C.

The author was born in Lviv, Ukraine in 1934. In his youth, he attended schools in the Ukraine, Poland, Czechoslovakia and Austria. In 1949, he immigrated with his parents, brother and sister to the United States. The author graduated from the City College of New York with a Bachelors of Mechanical Engineering degree in 1957 and received a Masters of Public Administration degree from the University of Northern Colorado in 1976. The author has traveled widely in Europe, South America and Canada. His personal interests are in the areas of world history and world affairs, and he has read numerous books on these subjects.

"Will Ukraine Bloom Again?" is the author's second book. The first book, "The Wind Blows to the East" published by Author House in 2005, accurately predicted the rise of China to superpower status in East Asia and the onset of the Islamic terrorism.

The author's father, Bohdan Dzerovych, was a prominent lawyer and judge in Lviv, Ukraine. He served as Lieutenant in the Ukrainian Regiment of the Austro-Hungarian Army during World War I. He was the Deputy Minister of Justice in the government of the Ukrainian State in 1941.

The author has two daughters, Daina and Stephanie. He also has four beautiful granddaughters, Mia, Emma, Reese and Aria and a handsome grandson, Owen.

Printed in the United States
By Bookmasters